LUCKY
MOUSE

BY ELIZABETH RING
PHOTOGRAPHS
BY DWIGHT KUHN

The Millbrook Press
Brookfield, Connecticut

E.R.: To my mother, Annice
D.K.: To my daughter, Anne

Several of the photographs and portions of the text of this book appeared in
Ranger Rick, a National Wildlife Federation magazine for children, in July 1992.

Library of Congress Cataloging-in-Publication Data
Ring, Elizabeth,
Lucky mouse / by Elizabeth Ring; photographs by Dwight Kuhn.
p. cm.
ISBN 1-56294-344-8
Summary: An orphaned deer mouse is found by children, placed in the nest of a
white-footed mouse, and raised as part of the white-footed mouse family.
1. Peromyscus—Juvenile literature. [1. White-footed mouse. 2. Mice.] I. Kuhn,
Dwight, ill. II. Title.
QL737.R666R56 1995
599.32'33—dc20   94-46948   CIP   AC

Published by The Millbrook Press, Inc.
2 Old New Milford Road
Brookfield, Connecticut 06804

A small mouse lies still at the side of the road, all
alone in the summer sun.

Some children saw the mouse tumble from the back of a truck that was loaded with logs.

"Lucky we saw her fall," Jennifer says.

"Is she alive?" asks Todd.

"Yes," says Chris. "Let's take her into the barn. We can put her in the nest with the white-footed mouse that has four baby mice of her own."

"Do you think the mother will take an orphan mouse in?" Lisa wonders.

"We can try," says Chris.

Soft little mouse. Hardly the size of one finger or thumb. She hasn't a clue that she's lost and alone.

There. Slip her into the nest while the mother mouse is outside. Look. She's just the same color, same size, same age: Her eyes are still closed—like the others. What will the mother mouse do when she sees one extra gray-and-white pup?

Listen! (*scribble-scrabble*) Shhhh. Here she comes now. The mother stops short and stares, as if asking herself: "What's this strange little one doing in *my* nest?! Her quivering nose checks the baby mouse from head to toe. *Will* she mother a mouse not her own?

Then, as if saying "Well, okay, I guess," the mother mouse abruptly lies down. Right away, her pups start to nurse.

The orphan mouse, too, butts her nose toward a nipple. At last, she connects and holds tight with her small greedy mouth. The nest is now full of tiny squeaks and soft sucking sounds.

Days go by. An orphan no more, the baby, it seems, has really become one of the white-footed mouse family. She has a warm place to be, four more pups to snuggle close to, and a mother to care for her. She shares in all the daily routines. At bath time, she, too, is groomed . . .

. . . in the same way the mother mouse cleans her own pups and herself—picking and licking, combing every inch of sleek fur, over body and face, into ears, everyplace.

The mother hunts nightly—for fruits, grasses, insects, nuts, and whatever else she finds tasty outside. Sometimes she finds people's food as well as things that grow wild. The pups thrive on the milk her well-fed body supplies.

How fast the young grow! In no time at all, they're bouncing all over the nest, tumbling over each other, and playing tag, hide-and-seek—even trouncing the mother mouse, who seems so patient with all their small games. The pups chirp, peep, squeal, and trill. Sometimes they buzz—like little bees.

Before long, the nest is a mess: lumpy and smelly and damp. No place for nice healthy mice to be!

The mother mouse sets to work to build a new nest, and when it is done, she carries the pups, one by one, in her mouth (as a cat carries kittens) to their new clean home. (She'll do this over and over before the pups are out on their own.)

Three weeks old, and the frisky pups are already exploring outdoors—sometimes with the mother mouse, sometimes alone. At each scary new sound, they scurry for home. In their fourth week, the mother's nursing is done. Now they all must find food by themselves. Will they find enough good things to eat? Will they survive?

No pup is more bent on exploring than the lively adopted one! She's in and out of the barn all night long. On each trip outside, she sniffs the air, and her beady black eyes search the sky and the ground. Her disklike ears twist this way and that, telling her where other night creatures are. And she twitches her whiskers (sideways and ahead) to feel her way around bushes and rocks—the way people reach out their arms when they can't see well in the dark.

She is, by far, the friskiest mouse in the bunch. Like a gymnast, she gallops and skips, sprints and springs.

And sometimes, full of excitement, she acts like a tap dancer—drumming her feet on the ground.

Look at her go! Her long tail helps her balance her body as she scampers, dives, bounces, and leaps.

She finds mushrooms and apples and acorns to eat. She gobbles up insects and grubs from the garden and around the roots of bushes and trees. One night she discovers her first juicy snail. She often nibbles on seeds and berries.

One night her keen nose leads her straight
through a hole in the pantry wall, where someone
has left the peanut butter spoon out on a shelf.
What a great sticky treat!

Just eight weeks old and, it seems, she is looking a *bit* different from the rest of the pups. For one thing, her tail is longer than the other pups' tails. What could this mean?

A week or so more goes by, and it's easy to see: More changes are taking place. Her fur is turning a fine velvety brown—like a deer's. It's not the shiny red-brown coat that white-footed mice wear. She must be a deer mouse! Does this mean she's no longer part of the white-footed mouse family?

Not at all. It just means she's a close cousin to her white-footed kin. She lives in the nest with the rest of the pups until they all leave to find homes of their own—each going its own separate way.

Like the others, the deer mouse travels worn paths along walls, around rocks, under roots, on her own secret trails. She won't stray too far from the barn as she inspects burrows, squirrels' and birds' nests, hollows in trees and logs. She searches a long time for a cozy, safe hideaway to live alone in for a while.

At last she chooses a burrow at the base of a tree. She lives out the winter there, snug in a nest she builds just for herself.

When nuts and berries become scarce, she gnaws the bark off the apple tree . . . which she can easily do with her sharp little front teeth that wear down as she gnaws. But, like a person's fingernails and hair, they grow all the time.

So, as she gnaws, her teeth stay the same length.

She never leaves home without a fast check—north and south, east and west. There are many hungry creatures to watch out for —and they are always on the lookout for *her!*

There's the fat prowling cat that stalks across fields and lawns on soft paws that hide its quick claws. It crouches and waits—and waits and waits—ready to pounce on any half-awake mouse.

In the woods near the barn lives the old saw-whet owl.
It hears every faint rustling sound on the ground, and it
peers all around with its big night-piercing eyes. On swift,
silent wings, it swoops down to clamp its talons on any
small animals that don't duck in time to escape.

And, all winter long, the weasel, camouflaged in its
snow-white coat, can easily leap in one bound to catch a
wee mouse . . . unless the mouse dives into a burrow too
tight for a weasel to follow.

This mouse, though, lasts the winter out. And, in the spring, she mates with a buck—a male deer mouse that's exactly her type. In an old hollow tree she nimbly builds a new nest of grasses and leaves, bits of paper, a soft feather or two—just like the nests the white-footed mouse mother made. Here is a safe home for her first deer mouse family.

With luck, the deer mouse will live a year, perhaps two—long enough to raise several more broods. She's been lucky before. Maybe she's going to be lucky again and again.

At least that's what the kids—who rescued her and watched her grow up in the warm barn—hope she will do.

If You Want to Know More About Mice

Q: Where did the name "mouse" come from?

A: "Mouse" comes from *mus*, a Sanskrit word that means "thief." It probably was chosen because mice "stole" grains and garden plants. All mice are rodents (from *rodere*, which means "to gnaw"in Latin.) All mice gnaw.

Q: Where do deer mice and white-footed mice live?

A: They live in North and South America, in forests, grasslands, deserts, and swamps—but mostly in forests.

Q: What is the difference between a deer mouse and a white-footed mouse?

A: Besides its color (soft brown instead of red-brown) and (in New England, at least) its longer tail with a little tuft of hair at its end, a deer mouse often has softer fur and larger ears. But the two look very much alike. In some places, white-footed mice are called deer mice—or wood mice, or vesper mice. A naturalist can tell the difference—but not always easily. Some scientists examine the skulls of mice and test mouse spit to more accurately tell one kind of mouse from another.

Q: What do baby mice look like when they are born?

A: Much different from the way they look at two weeks (the age of the deer mouse when it was adopted). They are all blind, deaf, toothless, pink-skinned and hairless, and their toes are stuck together. They are about the size of a grasshopper and weigh only about 1/25 of an ounce (1 gram).

Q: How big is a grown deer mouse?

A: About 6 inches (15 centimeters) from the tip of its nose to the end of its tail.

Q: Does a mouse really "sing"?

A: Yes, it chirps and twitters like a bird. A deer mouse is one of the best vocalists, but some white-footed mice sing, too.

Q: What does a mouse do best: hear, see, smell, taste, or feel?

A: Its sense of smell, which helps a mouse find its way along trails, recognize friends and enemies, and find a mate, is sharpest.

Q: How does a mouse use its sense of smell to find its way?

A: A mouse marks its trail with its urine and then follows the trail with its nose and with scent glands on the soles of its paws.

Q: How well can a mouse hear?

A: Very well. It can hear high-pitched sounds people can't hear at all.

Q: Does a father mouse ever live with its mate or its family?

A: Not often. The father and mother usually meet briefly to mate and then go their own ways. A father mouse may have many families. Sometimes, in winter, a male and a female may share a nest to keep warm. So may two males or two females.

Q: How many families does one mother mouse raise in a year?

A: Two to four—with anywhere between four and seven pups in each litter. Most litters are born in the spring and the fall. Sometimes a mother mouse mates shortly after a litter is born and is carrying a new family while she is caring for a half-grown one.

Q: How does a mother mouse protect her young?

A: Her nests are in hideaways; but, out of the nest, she will risk her own life to fight off enemies by jumping at them and baring her sharp teeth. If a baby mouse falls out of the nest, the mother mouse rescues it and carries it back home.

Q: How does a mother mouse carry her babies from one place to another?

A: One by one, much as a mother cat does. She picks a pup up in her mouth—sometimes by its neck, sometimes by its middle.

Q: How does a mother mouse get her young to go out on their own?

A: She doesn't drive them away. She herself may leave the nest, perhaps to make a new nest for a new family. Whenever the mother stops nursing them, the young mice search for their own food and shelter and start a new life.

Q: How far does a young mouse go to find a new home?

A: A female will go about 300 feet (90 meters) from home (not much farther than a city block). A male will range a bit farther.

Q: How many mice may live on one acre?

A: Maybe 4, maybe 20. Except when they are mating, they usually stay out of each other's way. Many young mice join the community during the summer. But probably just as many are eaten by other animals or die of some mouse disease.

Q: Does a deer mouse or a white-footed mouse ever live in a house?

A: Sometimes, if it can't find a nesting place outdoors. But most mice that live in houses are "house mice"—not as clean or as shy or as big as deer mice and white-footed mice.

Q: Does a deer mouse or white-footed mouse hibernate?

A: No, though it sleeps more in winter than in the summer.

Q: How many enemies does a mouse have?

A: Dozens. Besides, cats, owls, and weasels, a mouse has to run from such hungry creatures as skunks, coyotes, foxes, badgers, snakes, buzzards, kestrels, gulls, and even snapping turtles.

Q: How fast can a mouse run?

A: Over 7 miles (11 kilometers) an hour—when it's running from an enemy. It can jump about seven times its own length.

Q: Does a mouse hoard food?

A: Yes. Just as a squirrel hides food in the fall, a mouse stores food in logs, trees, or in the ground. Like a chipmunk, a mouse can carry about a teaspoon of berries or seeds in its cheeks. It carries nuts one at a time.

Q: Are deer mice and white-footed mice "pests"?

A: They can be—like Peter Rabbit—when they nibble on young plants, and some carry diseases or deer ticks that can cause disease. But they do not do the damage that meadow mice do. They are actually helpers in the way they eat many kinds of insect pests such as snails and slugs.

Q: Do deer mice and white-footed mice make good pets?

A: They can. But they are wild animals and belong in their natural habitats—as the children who rescued the deer mouse knew. Domesticated rodents, such as white mice, gerbils, hamsters, and guinea pigs, often make fine pets. And they have little chance of surviving in the wild.

About the Author and Photographer

Freelance editor and author Elizabeth Ring has written extensively for young readers, and natural history topics have often been the focus of her work. A former teacher and an editor at *Ranger Rick*, she has written a range of programs on environmental subjects for the National Wildlife Federation. Her previous books for the The Millbrook Press include two biographies, *Rachel Carson: Caring for the Earth* and *Henry David Thoreau: In Step With Nature*, as well as the *Good Dogs!* series, and, most recently, *Night Flier,* a picture book with photographs by Dwight Kuhn. She lives in Woodbury, Connecticut.

Photographer Dwight Kuhn is well known for his studes of nature subjects, expecially the beautifully composed close-ups that have appeared often in *Ranger Rick, World, National Geographic, Natural History*, and other magazines. Among his previous books for children are four that were named Outstanding Science Trade Books by the National Science Teachers Association and the Children's Book Council: *The Hidden Life of the Meadow, The Hidden Life of the Pond, The Hidden Life of the Forest,* and *More Than Just a Vegtable Garden.* He lives in Dexter, Maine.